MINIMUM WAGE TO MILLIONAIRE!

Minimum Wage to Millionaire!

How to Get Rich Cheap

Lorianne Holt

Writers Club Press
San Jose New York Lincoln Shanghai

Minimum Wage to Millionaire!
How to Get Rich Cheap

Writers Club Press
an imprint of iUniverse.com, Inc.

For information address:
iUniverse.com, Inc.
5220 S 16th, Ste. 200
Lincoln, NE 68512
www.iuniverse.com

ISBN: 0-595-14993-6

Printed in the United States of America

Dedication

First, I want to dedicate this book to all of you working hard to attain financial independence. I want to do everything I can to help you to become a success! In addition, I would like to dedicate this book to my family: Ruth, Kimberli, Stephany, Bryan, Anthony, Jenefer, Matthew, and Angalina, all of whom love me so much, and let me know it!

List of Tables

Foreword

This publication was designed to provide accurate information of a general and current nature only. It is published under the express understanding that neither the writer nor the publisher has the specific background in or is engaged in rendering legal, accounting, or other professional services. Any information, therefore, should be evaluated in the context of each individual's particular and unique financial circumstances. The services of competent legal and accounting professionals should be sought and consulted before implementing any strategies outlined here.

It is also assumed that tax laws and economic dynamics change on a constant basis, and other uncontrollable factors may limit or even prohibit the use of certain investment options or financial planning strategies.

Since a basic financial education is desirable and helpful to begin self-reliance and empowerment toward financial independence, this book was developed as a helpful tool and basic building block upon which to develop additional personal money management, financial planning, and investing skills.

Preface

This book is a must for anyone who realizes that there can be more that they can personally do to better their position in life. This book can inform and encourage anyone to become financially successful from all walks of life, including high school students, college students, minimum wage earners, middle income earners, displaced or laid-off workers, unemployed persons, welfare recipients, persons with disabilities, and retired persons. If you are in any of these categories, you can use the information found in this book to literally change your life for the better. You can become successful, too!

My hope is that you will take this information and apply it to your absolute best advantage, carefully and wisely!

Acknowledgements

First thing, I want to give thanks to our Supreme Being for Her goodness and for Her many blessings, which She has generously bestowed upon me and my family.

I want to give special thanks to my partner, Ruth Sanchez, for her many excellent suggestions, her strong belief in me, and her excitement over this project. Her input for this book was invaluable!

Introduction

Have you heard the loud bumping sounds echoing across America these days? Those bumping sounds you may be hearing are millions of Americans doing one or more of these three things: They're bumping their heads upon the cement ceiling of low wages; they're bumping their bottoms upon the concrete floor of a lowered standard of living; and they're thumping their fists against the hard wall of total frustration, wondering why they can't get ahead!

It's been stated recently that for every hour you work a job, 25 minutes of that hour is going to pay taxes. 18 minutes is worked so that your boss can make money. And overhead comes to another 8 minutes. So, as a result, you only get to keep 9 minutes out of every hour worked for yourself. It's no wonder that you may feel poorer literally every second!

It used to be so simple. Go to school. Get a job. Save money. Work until you retire. Retire. Die happy and fulfilled. But now, things have changed a lot. Our out-dated school system has not caught up to the razor-sharp realities of our new economy. Today's wage-earner needs to know how to obtain and use whatever money they can earn to its highest and best potential. You can't afford to be complacent anymore, nor can you afford to be ignorant about the use of money if you want to get ahead and have the things you want out of life.

It is a terrible shame that you can spend the first quarter of your life in school, yet leave knowing nothing about money, except how to spend it! Your parents never figured it out, or you would have been born with a silver spoon in your mouth (I didn't even get a slightly-used spoon). Most people know very little about how to obtain and use the most sought-after commodity in the world.

I've learned about finances the hard way, through life experiences, and I would like to let you in on some of what I have learned, for those of you who, most likely, will choose not get within ten feet of the traditional, thick, heavy financial volume.

What you are about to read is a bare-bones, down-to-earth explanation and initiation on how you can become financially healthy, wealthy, and wise on a low budget. There are so many books out there that can tell you how to achieve financial independence, but they are written and geared to those who make a considerable amount of money over and above the poverty line. Have you ever noticed that they never really tell you how they got that first investment money, in the first place? Their perspective is so sophisticated that they can't see below a certain financial level, which is, I assure you, certainly higher than yours, at this point.

I have read these treasure troves of financial information over and over again, always looking for something that would apply to my financial situation (broke and barely making it). I became frustrated that being broke meant that I could not enter into the financial environment I was getting so excited about.

I have always loved studying financial investing and money strategies. Let's say that I've been somewhat of a fanatic about it. I have read every book I could get my hands on about money. We all know that having money is power, and I wanted to become powerful over my own financial circumstances. I didn't want outside and unpredictable events to continue to overwhelm and dominate the lives of my family and myself.

This book will show you how to plan and make goals for your financial future. You will also be shown how to appreciate and enjoy the good things that life has to offer right now, wherever you are financially.

The whole premise of this book is based upon the lowest legal amount (as of August 2000) that you can earn on a job—minimum wage. This is where most people start their working life. High school students, college students, wage-earners and retired workers can benefit from the advice given in these pages. Even those who have already been in the workforce, but who have been forced to start over again, can use this book to better their financial situation.

This book has something for everybody at every stage of their financial life. It is my hope that the information contained in this book will help open your mind and free you from old brainwashed, tired ideas, as well as help you to see yourself taking control of your life, powerfully and optimistically. No matter what anyone may say, your life, including your financial well-being, is firmly in your grasp!

Good Luck!

(If you are further down the road financially, or you want to go further in a shorter period of time, take a look at Chapter 12, New Ideas. In this chapter, there is information on a new program that offers unsecured, non-qualifying loans of $10,000 or $20,000, your choice, for any purpose, at 6% interest, no credit necessary. Included in this program is membership in a non-profit home ownership association that will provide 100% financing for your own home and/or real estate investments, for as low as 3% interest, up to $5,000,000, no qualifying. Check it out! It just may provide the powerful step up you need to succeed!)

Contents

Chapter 1

Real Life Cash Flow

"Wealth is when small efforts produce big results.
Poverty is when big efforts produce small results."
~George David, M.D.

Do you like where you are financially? Would you like to achieve control and even dominance over your financial life?

I have always wanted to be rich. I used to study the following hot topics: how to become rich overnight; how to invest and make a fortune immediately; how to own half of North America by Tuesday; so forth and so on. Obviously, nothing in this life works that easy. So, after spending tons of money and wasting years on get-rich-quick schemes, I settled down and began to think about what I really wanted out of life. In my case, I wanted money so I could, one day, live life leisurely, doing exactly what I wanted to do, every day, 365 days of the year. I wanted money to enjoy the good things life has to offer (i.e. travel, entertainment, good food, etc.). I wanted money so I wouldn't have to be dependent on any government agency (i.e. welfare, Social Security, and other forms of government aid). And, last but certainly not least, I wanted money so that my children could live comfortably now, and for the rest of their lives, as well. I think that most people would agree that these goals are reasonable and shared by most average Americans. But are they realistic for someone with a low income? If so, how?

First, let's define "low income". The American government describes the poverty level at approximately $14,244 per year for a family of four. That amounts to a working couple, both earning at minimum wage, with 28% in taxes already taken out. That $14,244 a year is the amount, after taxes, the couple with two children must live on successfully.

As a divorced, single parent with six children, I had to rely on welfare in order to make ends meet. Many times, most months, I had only $10 left to myself after I paid all of our household expenses. I look at my old budgets, written in spiral notebooks, and I don't know how we made it, but somehow, some way, we did, with help from government agencies, and occasional help from relatives. Without following my budget strictly, we would have been in even greater trouble. Our family was the epitome of "low income", so I know what I'm talking about. Thankfully, those days are long gone now, and I have accomplished many goals towards my dream of financial independence, including doing exactly what I want to do, 365 days of the year, and enjoying the good life. If I can do it, you certainly can too!

In order for you to become financially successful on a minimum wage income, you have to become **very serious about your priorities.** It is very easy to forget about your goals when they seem to be so far into the future. You have only two choices in front of you: either you have to make every penny of what you take in (income) count in your favor, or, you have to lower your outgo (expenses). **You have no other alternatives. You must live within your income in order to survive and do well financially.**

I know that you have heard this before, but you really do have to make a real life cash flow plan (a budget) in order to figure out where the money is going to. A sample plan would look like this:

Minimum Wage Income
2-Wage Couple
$5.15/hour x 2 earners = $10.30/hour Gross
$10.30/hour x 160 hours = $1,648/month Gross
$1,648/month—$461/month taxes @ 28% = $1,187/month Net
Net Yearly Amount Available = $14,244

Net Monthly Income: $1,187

Expenses*:

Rent (2 bedroom apartment)	$450
Electric bill	50
Gas company bill	26
Food bill	200
Phone Bill (basic)	20
Cable TV bill (basic)	30
Gasoline	80
Car Insurance (min. collision)	30
Hair/Clothes, incl. laundry	40
Misc. Paper Goods, incl. soap	15
Checking account service charge	10
Entertainment	80
Car Maintenance (save for registration and repairs)	32

Total Expenses*: $1,087
Money left over for saving/investing: $124

*Of course, all amounts are estimates, as an example only. In some areas, some expenses are higher, some are lower, and some don't exist, for your personal situation, as a category. I just want you to get used to using a budget to keep track of your spending.

You probably think that I may be nitpicking about some of these expenses, but you have to count everything you spend money on. It all adds up, no matter how small the amount!

You may have noticed that there are no items in this sample budget that are credit-related. That's absolutely right! Having credit at this time is the biggest detriment to financial responsibility there is. There is no room for credit at this level, in any amount. Learn to pay cash for everything. I know that it's old-fashioned, but this is where you are right now. I am assuming that you already own a car, either given to you, or bought with saved funds. If you don't really need a car, or if you can use a bus for some of your transportation, you will save more money to be used for your financial goals.

If you make more than the minimum wage level, you can use some credit sparingly, but only to start a good credit record, nothing more. Don't let anyone tell you that you absolutely have to have credit to survive! There are so many people having financial difficulties, even filing for bankruptcy, that the economic system is having to adapt in order to continue selling consumer products and goods. Even with bad credit, or no credit, you can buy just about anything, including real estate. And don't forget, cash is still king!

If you are single, and the first plan does not apply to you, here is a plan for you:

Minimum Wage—Single Person
$5.15/hour x 160 hours = $824/month Gross
$824/month—$230/month taxes @ 28% = $594/month Net
Net Yearly Amount Available = $7,128

Net Monthly Income: $594
Expenses*:

Rent (live with roommate)	$200
Electric bill (share 1/2)	25
Gas company bill (share 1/2)	14
Food bill	80
Phone bill (basic, share 1/2)	10
Cable TV bill (basic, share 1/2)	15
Bus Pass	30
Hair/Clothes, incl. laundry	30
Misc. Paper Goods, incl. soap	10
Checking account service charge	10
Entertainment	80

Total Expenses*: $504
Money left over for saving/investing: $90
*Of course, all amounts are estimates, as an example only. In some areas, some expenses are higher, some are lower, and some don't exist, for your personal situation, as a category. I just want you to get used to using a budget to keep track of your spending.

With both plans, it appears you have a little money left over at the end of the month. Not bad. Better than zero, and much better than minus zero, which is like most people who usually have more month than money. If you have children, their expenses, including child care, have not been figured into the budgets, which is a major consideration.

It's not easy taking care of children on a minimum wage budget, but people manage it somehow everyday. Entertainment is flexible in these budgets. You can save up for a big amusement park day or find cheaper entertainment every week. You should have a fun outlet on a regular basis so you won't feel like things are so tight. Later on in this book, there are suggestions on things to do for fun that don't cost very much. It doesn't take a lot of money to have fun, especially if you happen to like the company you are inviting to go with you. So go out regularly and have fun!

Now, back to the money left over at the end of the month. What do you want to do with it? Your best bet is to invest it, make it grow more money for you. A little money now will go a long way, if saved now for the future. How to do this effectively will be covered in Chapter Two, Investing on a Budget.

Notes

Chapter 2

Investing on a Budget

*"Money is the seed of money, and the first guinea
is sometimes more difficult to acquire
than the second million."*
~Jean Jacques Rousseau

In Chapter One, Real Life Cash Flow, we prepared two plans to illustrate typical financial situations. You will notice that there was money left over in both plans. Let's see what we can do with it.

For the single plan, you had $90 left over after expenses. I suggest you put $24/mo. into an emergency fund, and $16/mo. into a retirement investment program. Then, put the $50/mo. you have left into a no-load stock mutual fund. Read on for more on these investing details.

If you are in a couple, you had $124 left over after expenses. As a working couple, you'll want to purchase low-cost Term life insurance. Term life insurance will protect your family from loss of income resulting from the untimely death of one or both of the wage-earners. Term life insurance is preferred over Whole life insurance or Universal life insurance because Term life insurance is straight insurance, no investment products added. Whole life insurance or Universal life insurance gives a death benefit and comes with investment products that are obtained through the issuing life insurance company. You will find that it is cheaper to obtain just Term life insurance, and invest on your own, rather than to rely on their investment strategies, which often give you a poorer return on your investment than you can get for yourself. Life insurance should not be considered a financial investment. It is security and protection for your family. A good company to contact for life insurance quotes is Insurance Quote Services at (800) 972-1104.

A Term life insurance policy of $125,000 per working adult is inexpensive, and should be sufficient at this point. If you are under 40 years old and a non-smoker, the insurance should cost around $12 per month each, which is $24 to add to your budget. After adding $24 in life insurance to the budget, you have $100 left. Take $34 and put it into an emergency fund. Most people don't have emergencies every month, and, if they do, hopefully there is someone from whom they can borrow from that can wait to be paid back a bit at a time. Now you have $66 left. Put $16 into a retirement investment fund. All $16 of it. It doesn't look like much now, but wait until you consider the facts: $16/mo. invested at 10% interest for 40 years will grow to $100,000. If you are age 25, your $16/mo. would total $7,680 in total contributions over 40 years. Time and compound interest (compounded monthly) would turn that amount into $100,000 by age 65. Kind of amazing, isn't it? Now, what about the $50 left? Invest it in a no-load (no sales charge) stock mutual fund and watch it grow!

Here are the details of the retirement and stock mutual fund investments. You invest the $16 for your retirement investment program in a tax-deferred flexible premium annuity for your old age. Tax-deferred means you don't pay taxes on the increase of your money until you withdraw it at retirement age. You don't pay any taxes on tax-deferred annuities, so your money grows untouched (except for a low yearly management cost that is deducted from the account). You may invest any amount, even as low as $10, if you can't afford more. The source for the tax-deferred flexible premium annuity is listed in Chapter 10, Retirement.

The no-load stock mutual fund investment will allow your money to work for you. You can save in this manner for large expenditures, such as a home, schooling, vacations, etc. Your mutual fund investment will pay you more than a regular bank savings account, and you can access it just as easily.

There are many mutual fund families to choose from, but my personal favorite, for ease of investing and excellent customer service, is American Century Investments. They have no-load funds that are consistent and well-managed. The usual opening investment is $2,500, but they will allow you to start with $50 if you allow them to use automatic monthly debits from your checking account to invest. The minimum monthly automatic investment amount is $50. For more information on this family of funds, call (800) 345-2021 and ask for a prospectus.

Over the years, one of the steadiest vehicles for the appreciation of investment funds has been company stocks. Amazingly enough, if you had been alive on January 1, 1897, with $10,000 to invest in a group of common stock that was linked to the Dow Jones Industrial Average (the oldest and most widely quoted stock market indicator), you would have had, by the end of 1993, 97 years later, with all dividends reinvested and no taxes considered, $112,208,600, at an average percent return of

10.08%. This is a truly amazing testimony to the value of stock market investing!

There is a lot of enjoyment in the science and art of picking individual stocks of companies that you may be familiar with, like McDonald's, Procter & Gamble, IBM, etc. For those of you who have the time and inclination to research individual companies for their earnings and growth potential, I recommend that you read the good books available that can instruct you in your investment interests. But, if you don't want the headaches and stress of learning when to buy and sell individual stocks effectively, I suggest that you invest your money in stocks through a good stock mutual fund.

A stock mutual fund is a pool of stock shares from different companies bought with investor funds, managed by the professionals employed by an investment company. The investment company belongs to the shareholders, not to management. The same investment advice that used to belong only to large investors is now being made available to the small investor, in a mutual fund.

Let's use a couple of graphs to help you to figure out your investment capabilities at 10% interest:

Value of Investing $1.00
Each Month at 10%*

Year	Amount Invested	Account Value	Year	Amount Invested	Account Value
1	12	$12.54	36	432	3,751.21
2	24	26.34	37	444	4,138.87
3	36	41.51	38	456	4,565.30
4	48	58.20	39	468	5,034.37
5	60	76.56	40	480	5,550.35
6	72	96.76	41	492	6,117.92
7	84	118.97	42	504	6,742.26
8	96	143.41	43	516	7,429.02
9	108	170.29	44	528	8,184.47

10	120	199.86	45	540	9,015.45
11	132	232.39	46	552	9,929.54
12	144	268.17	47	564	10,935.03
13	156	307.53	48	576	12,041.08
14	168	350.82	49	588	13,257.72
15	180	398.44	50	600	14,596.04
16	192	450.83	51	612	16,068.18
17	204	508.45	52	624	17,687.54
18	216	571.84	53	636	19,468.84
19	228	641.56	54	648	21,428.26
20	240	718.26	55	660	23,583.63
21	252	802.63	56	672	25,954.53
22	264	895.43	57	684	28,562.52
23	276	997.51	58	696	31,431.31
24	288	1,109.80	59	708	34,586.99
25	300	1,233.32	60	720	38,058.23
26	312	1,369.20	61	732	41,876.59
27	324	1,518.66	62	744	46,076.79
28	336	1,683.06	63	756	50,697.01
29	348	1,863.91	64	768	55,779.25
30	360	2,062.84	65	780	61,369.71
31	372	2,281.67			
32	384	2,522.38			
33	396	2,787.15			
34	408	3,078.41			
35	420	3,398.79			

*Compounded annually. To figure your investment amount, multiply the Account Value of the year you choose by your yearly investment amount.

Value of Investing

$1.00 ONCE at 10%*

Year	Account Value	Year	Account Value
1	$1.10	36	30.91
2	1.21	37	34.00
3	1.33	38	37.40
4	1.46	39	41.14
5	1.61	40	45.26
6	1.77	41	49.79
7	1.95	42	54.76
8	2.14	43	60.24
9	2.36	44	66.26
10	2.59	45	72.89
11	2.85	46	80.18
12	3.14	47	88.20
13	3.45	48	97.02
14	3.80	49	106.72
15	4.18	50	117.39
16	4.59	51	129.13
17	5.05	52	142.04
18	5.56	53	156.25
19	6.12	54	171.87
20	6.73	55	189.06
21	7.40	56	207.97
22	8.14	57	228.76
23	8.95	58	251.64
24	9.85	59	276.80
25	10.83	60	304.48
26	11.92	61	334.93
27	13.11	62	368.42

28	14.42	63	405.27
29	15.86	64	445.79
30	17.45	65	490.37
31	19.19		
32	21.11		
33	23.23		
34	25.55		
35	28.10		

*Compounded annually. To figureyour investment amount, multiply the Account Value of the year you choose by your investment amount.

The following graph shows the rates of annual growth necessary to compound various amounts into $1,000,000:

Starting Cash	5 yrs.	10 yrs.	15 yrs.	20 yrs.	25 yrs.	30 yrs.
$100,000	59%	26%	17%	12%	10%	8%
75,000	68	30	19	14	11	9
50,000	82	35	22	16	13	11
40,000	90	38	24	18	14	11
30,000	102	42	26	19	15	12
20,000	119	48	30	22	17	14
10,000	151	59	36	26	20	17
5,000	189	70	42	30	24	19
4,000	202	74	45	32	25	20
3,000	220	79	47	34	26	21
2,000	247	86	51	36	28	23
1,000	298	100	59	41	32	26

As you can see, it is your best interests to invest, and make the money that you have worked hard to obtain, now work for you! You can't let a low monthly income keep you from making the attempt to better your financial situation. No matter how small the amount of money you start with, time and a high rate of compound interest can work wonders for you. Take advantage of these factors now!

As a further incentive to invest, I want to give you two realistic examples of what the average minimum wage earner, with determination, can accomplish. In the first example, let me emphasize that you don't need a lot of money to get started investing. You can invest as little as $50 a month and become a millionaire in about 40 years.

According to a recent poll of high school juniors and seniors, they reported that they waste at least $15 to $20 a week on things they don't really need—snacks, candy, video games, etc. That totals $60 to $80 a month, or $720 to $960 a year. If that much money passes through kids' hands each month, think of how much adults must waste! Many adults say they waste much more!

If you could harness at least $50 a month and use it to start a regular investing program, you could be well on your way to becoming a millionaire!

If you invested that $50/mo. in a growth stock mutual fund, and your money grew at 13% to 15% annually, which is very likely, your portfolio, if you leave it untouched, would be worth a great deal over the long term:

> After 10 years: $12,500 to $14,000
> After 20 years: $54,900 to $70,700
> After 30 years: $198,000 to $300,000
> After 40 years: $817,700 to $1,570,000

A little bit of money, time and compound interest works like a charm every time!

In our next example, let's suppose that our average minimum wage earner (AMWE for short) decided, at age 20, to devote only ten years of his working life, starting now, to becoming a millionaire by age 65. AMWE supplements his regular earnings by working a part-time job, or operating a small sideline business, or living rent-free with someone, etc., in order to sacrifice and save $180 a month for his goal. Most young AMWEs sacrifice at this age to save for credit-related items and toys (stereo systems, cars, partying, clothes, etc.) Our AMWE has decided that all of those things can wait for ten years. (Interesting concept! Our AMWE must have a lot of courage to forgo these pleasures! I believe that he would actually work a little harder in order to have his fun **and** invest at the same time. I know that I would! Also, at this point in life, if you don't have any children, don't produce any. Life only gets harder financially in order to support them.) He knows that while his friends may think he's nuts for not joining in on the mad rush to consume and to gain the appearance of wealth, he knows that with diligence and persistence he will win in the end.

So, at age 20, our AMWE has decided to invest $180 monthly into a tax-deferred flexible premium annuity until age 30. He chooses to place this money into the aggressive growth mutual fund option offered by the annuity plan, which has consistently grown approximately 20% per year. (Details on this annuity are in Chapter Ten, Retirement.) AMWE knows that no mutual fund can guarantee results, but he is only looking for at least a 10% yearly return on his money.

AMWE saves and invests with a determination and single-mindedness that shocks his family and friends, who can't understand why he is sacrificing so hard for such a far-away goal. AMWE understands the principles of money. He knows that time and compound interest will **always** reap a greater reward over and above the amount he has put in.

AMWE invests a total of $21,600 by age 30, earning approximately 10% appreciation yearly along the way, for a total of $35,974.80. Our AMWE allows his $35,974.80 to continue working for him, with no further investment on his part. Then, AMWE buys a bottle of champagne (he can afford it!), and celebrates his hard work and determination, because at age 65, without investing a single penny more, when all of his friends are trying to make ends meet at their retirement, AMWE will have $1,010,892 available to live on to show for his 10-year sacrifice.

AMWE will be able to receive **over $8,000 for living expenses monthly for the rest of his life,** from age 65 on! AMWE only sacrificed 10 years of his time for future financial independence. From age 30 on, he did not have to invest any more money into his plan, and by working so hard, he had so progressed in his working career that, by age 30, that $180/mo. he was putting away was not a strain on his budget, like it was when he first began his plan. AMWE came out the long distance winner! **Anyone can do this!**

If you started on this program from age 30 to age 40, you would need to invest $500/mo. to accrue over $1,000,000 by age 65. Obviously, the longer you wait to begin such a program means that more money must be saved and invested to accomplish the same goal. At any age, it is a wise policy to save and invest as much as possible. (In Chapter 12, New Ideas, if you haven't already looked, there are details on a new program that offers unsecured, no-qualifying loans of $10,000 or $20,000, at 6% interest, no credit necessary. You could use this money to fund your retirement investment plan, especially if you are starting out with your investments at a later age. What a novel idea!)

If you're not able to invest as much as the amounts given in our examples, keep in mind that most people can live just fine on the interest generated by a goal of $500,000 at retirement, which means cutting in half the investment amounts given in the above examples. Whatever amount you aim for, the main point is that there is no obstacle in your way to becoming a millionaire, if you start early and invest consistently!

Notes

Chapter 3

Credit

There is a time and a place for the judicious use of credit. Unfortunately, in this society, a good credit record can come in handy. It seems that you can't do anything without a credit record, of some kind. There is nothing wrong with some credit handled wisely, but credit handled unwisely is like holding a cobra by the tail, and hoping that you can dodge its head accurately enough so that it won't bite you. Most of the time, I assure you, you will lose the contest, big time. But, if credit is used very wisely, very carefully, you can stay ahead of the game, and win the prize, which is a responsible credit record.

The best recommendation, for someone just starting out, is to obtain a secured credit card. The way it works is like this: you are required to make a deposit of, say $400, into a savings account with the bank issuing the secured card, securing your credit line. The bank will give you a credit line of $400 on a Visa or Mastercard. The benefits are: you get the use of your money (although you are now paying interest on your own money, you are also earning interest on the money in your savings account); you can use the card as an emergency fund (don't spend it on consumer goods and food); and you can build up a good credit rating, by paying your monthly bill promptly. As an added security, if life gets ugly, and you have problems paying your bills, the secured savings account can be closed to get rid of at least one monthly bill, and the card will be paid off. One source for a secured credit card is First National Bank of Marin, P. O. Box 98874, Las Vegas, NV 89193-8874, (702) 269-1100. Other sources of secured credit cards can be found on the Internet. Just type "secured credit cards" into your chosen search engine, and you'll get multiple listings of available secured credit card offers.

Another use of credit is in the form of investment debt. Wisely used, investment debt can make you a wealthy person in a much more accelerated way, as long as your gains are higher than the cost of using debt to obtain them. In other words, borrowing money at 3% or 6% interest a month is a wise use of investment debt if your returns are 10%+per month, or your investment produces enough income to pay for the debt, as well as show you a profit. Borrowing money at 24% interest a month to invest at 10% is not a good idea. Just use your common sense and caution when utilizing debt to finance your investment dreams. Wise use of debt can make you a millionaire!

Notes

Chapter 4

Bankruptcy

"Progress always involves risk.
You can't steal second base
and keep your foot on first."
~Frederick B. Wilcox

The first thing I have to say is, if runaway credit debt is keeping you from investing in your future, don't wait too long to go bankrupt! It doesn't make any sense to lose everything by trying to look good and act as if nothing is wrong, when it definitely is! The worse enemy of your financial independence is the misuse and abuse of credit. If you are reading this book before you have had the chance to wrack up debts, then you're way ahead of the game! Now, your job is to stay determined to keep yourself free of credit misery. If you are reading this book after wracking up debts, for whatever reason, this chapter is for you. Your job is to jettison the debt. That's right. Dump it! Although the government is seeking ways to limit one's ability to go bankrupt, it is still perfectly legal to start over again, using bankruptcy. You have the legal right to reclaim control over your financial situation. The government is trying to limit bankruptcies by people who have the money to pay their bills. You're probably not in that position, and your first priority is to yourself and to your family. No one else cares about you and your family like you do! Your income is your only weapon in the fight against poverty. If all else fails, use bankruptcy to free your income!

What is bankruptcy? Bankruptcy is a way to get out of debt when you owe more money than you can be expected to pay in the near future. The law allows you to have a court "discharge" or cancel most of your debts in order to make a fresh start.

You can go bankrupt in one of two ways: either Chapter 7 or Chapter 13. Chapter 7 is straight bankruptcy. In my opinion, this is the best choice. Chapter 13 involves paying off your debts over time, at a much lower rate, under court supervision. You have to have a steady income, and owe less than $350,000 in secured debt and less than $100,000 in unsecured debt. In my experience, credit grantors view a Chapter 13 bankruptcy less favorably than Chapter 7 bankruptcy when granting you new credit. This is because you are still responsible for your old debts with a Chapter 13, and this is used against you when figuring your ratio of income to credit. Chapter 7 clears you from your previous debt, and you truly have no credit when you begin looking for new credit.

You can use bankruptcy to discharge your debts, no matter how you got into debt. Maybe you used your credit cards like crazy, and then realized your mistake. Perhaps you lost your job, and now you are unable to pay your bills. Credit problems can happen to the best of people. Use bankruptcy to your advantage!

Bankruptcy usually means that most, and sometimes all, of your debts will be canceled. And, except for debts that you must pay, going through bankruptcy generally stops your creditors from "garnishee-ing" or taking your wages. This means your employer cannot be forced to give part of your salary to your creditors to pay off your discharged debts.

Can bankruptcy be filed at any time? Yes, as long as your debts were not discharged less than six years ago. As soon as you file the proper bankruptcy forms in court, you can stop making payments on your unsecured debts, except for alimony and child support. Any debts secured by property cannot be discharged. Suppose you bought a car or a stereo system and signed an agreement promising the return of the property if you couldn't make the payments. In this case, you would not be allowed to cancel the debt and keep the property. You would have to either pay it off as promised or give it back in good condition.

The law says that creditors cannot garnishee your wages, sue you, or bother you with letters or telephone calls asking for payment. If they persist, tell them to check with the bankruptcy court. Legally they have to stop trying to collect, period.

How do you start? Go to a paralegal who can fill out the proper forms for you and tell you where to file them with the nearest U.S. Bankruptcy Court. Be careful to list all of your debts because if you make any mistakes, some or all of your debts might not be canceled. The court will tell you what the filing fee will be. There are many ads in the newspaper for the preparation of bankruptcy forms. They are usually low cost, and, if your debts are low and uncomplicated, you don't need an attorney to assist you, just a paralegal who can properly fill out the forms. This is called filing "pro per". It usually takes about 90 to 180 days for your debts to be discharged.

If you would like more information on bankruptcy, contact a paralegal specializing in bankruptcy, and get a copy of the bankruptcy procedures from your nearest State Bar Association. There are also some very good books on the subject in the library.

Notes

Chapter 5

Value Hints

"Give a man a fish and you feed him
for a day. Teach a man to fish
and you feed him for a lifetime."

~Lao Tzu

Now that you have the incentive to stick to your cash flow plan and have money left over to invest, you will need to learn how to be very thrifty, to get more bang for your buck. Here are some suggestions:

*Go out and find tag sales, thrift shops, end-of-season sales, used sporting equipment stores, newspaper ads, and friends getting rid of stuff. You'll find great bargains.

*Don't buy name brands, unless the generic is of proven poorer quality. Most generically labeled goods are of the same quality as the name brands, only cheaper.

*Clip store coupons for food, but only for the products you actually use. You can get coupons in most Sunday editions and in one weekly food edition of your daily newspaper.

*Don't drive all around town for food bargains. You're probably saving cents, but using dollars for the gas you're using. Find the store that offers the best overall prices in your area.

*Don't buy food you're not going to eat. Clean out your cupboards of unwanted food by donating it to a food bank. You'll have more room for what you will eat.

*Plan your dinner meals around vegetables, not meat. Add some pasta and grains, and only a very small portion of meat. You will feel satisfied and save a lot of money in your food budget.

*Plan a menu for the week. Go shopping only once a week. Do not shop for food everyday. Get to know your food costs, and stay within your food budget.

*Do not shop for food when you are hungry. This is self-defeating.

*Just because it says "sale" on it doesn't mean it is truly a bargain. Some stores actually increase the price of an item before putting it on "sale". Compare prices with other stores before you fall for this trick.

*Get your hair done at a beauty college. It is inexpensive, and the students are usually competent and supervised closely.

*Save on your utilities. Wear heavier clothes in the house when it is cold, and wear lighter clothing when it's hot.

*Don't watch TV everyday. Read, play games, talk, or listen to music instead. The TV gobbles up a lot of electricity. Try it for one month and see the difference in your electric bill.

Notes

Chapter 6

Money Smarts

"You can get everything in life you want...
if you'll just help enough other people
get what they want."

~Zig Ziglar

In order to maximize your cash flow, you can use the following suggestions to either increase your income or decrease your expenses:
  *Start a small business from a hobby. There are many excellent books on this subject in the library.

*Conduct garage or yard sales. It won't hurt to include a few new items in small quantities that you were able to acquire at a substantial discount through a merchandise distributor.

*Take care of disabled person in or out of your home. Contact your local Dept. of Public Social Services and become a part-time Home Health Aide. Many disabled people only need about 4 hours of care a day for household cleaning, shopping, cooking meals, doing errands, etc. These services can be performed before and after a regular job, and the job pays minimum wage. You'll be of great help, and you'll probably make a new friend.

*If you're handy with a hammer, become a Property Manager in an apartment complex. Live rent-free on the premises while keeping the tenants and the owner satisfied.

*Take an adult education class on minor car maintenance. You'll save a lot of money on minor car repairs.

*Recycle. Ask your friends and family to save their recyclables and arrange to pick them up on a weekly basis for recycling funds.

*Live with an elderly person. You can help each other share costs and provide each other with valuable companionship.

*Work a second job.

*If your job is relatively close to home and easy to get to, buy a bus pass and sell the car. For occasional outings, ride with someone else and share gas costs or rent a car for the occasion. You'll save on car maintenance, car insurance, and gasoline costs. Arrange to share a ride to the grocery store with a friend, relative, or neighbor, if needed.

*Use your imagination!

Notes

Chapter 7

Entertainment on a Budget

*"The man who does not work for the love of work
but only for money is not likely to make money,
nor to find much fun in life."*
~Charles M. Schwab

How can you have fun on a tight budget? There are many activities that have low or no admission fees that can be enjoyed by anyone, regardless of family size. Here is a secret: most of the money spent on an outing is spent on food and drink, which can add up to 2 to 3 times more than the cost to get there. Solution: bring your own food and drink everywhere, even to the amusement park. Here are some hints on things to do, places to go, and how to enjoy your outings:

*Outdoor activities. Most activities only need a minimum one-time investment in sports equipment, then you can play for free in most public facilities.

*Keep a pair of lawn chairs in your car trunk. You never know when you'll pass a beautiful place, where you can linger and sit down for a while.

*Visit local museums.

*Go to local parks. In many parks, they have free concerts or theatre events. Call your local Parks and Recreation department for details.

*Enjoy listening to books on tape. You can get them from your local library.

*Host a potluck block party. Get to know your neighbors.

*Create a garden, either indoors or outdoors.

*Go out to a dance club before cover starts. This will give you a chance to talk to friends before the music gets too loud, besides saving the cover charge, which can be expensive.

*If you want to go to the movies, go to the early matinees. They are usually half the regular price.

*Go on a picnic at a bird or wildlife sanctuary.

*Get a group of friends over and sing. Karaoke tapes are inexpensive, and can be played on a regular tape player or stereo system.

*Sit back, and listen to your favorite music.

*Make a dinner date with your significant other at least once a month, or sooner.

*Take up an inexpensive hobby.

*Hang out with your friends.

*Join a local theater group. It's a great way to meet people.

*Learn a foreign language. There are many taped programs that really work.

*If you love to cook, get together with others who love to cook also, and take turns creating great, low-cost dinners, once a month.

*Start or join a reading group. There are great books available to read and talk about.

*Visit your local library. Continue your education for free.

*Play cards with family and friends. If you have children, this is a good time to teach them to play card games, and also a good opportunity to socialize with them.

*Play board games for the same reasons as above.

*Rent videos at the library. Pop some popcorn. Enjoy!

*Use your imagination. Have fun!

Notes

Chapter 8

Schooling and Careers

*"If money is your hope for independence you will
never have it. The only real security that man
can have in this world is a reserve of knowledge,
experience and ability."*

~Henry Ford

The best kind of schooling, in my humble opinion, is life experience, but unfortunately, that is not the way our educational system is set up. The present system rewards memorization skills, not actual knowledge. Many times, if you bring your years of school, your grade point average, and your newly-minted college diploma to a job interview, you will be asked, "Do you have any related work experience?". In most cases, you have been so busy making bills and going into debt over your education that you haven't had the opportunity to work or gain practical experience in your chosen field of study.

College is getting extremely expensive to attend, even for the wealthy. All across the country, schools are making it increasingly more difficult to earn college degrees. The traditional college student learns mainly concept and theory courses that are virtually useless in their professions. Why should you pay good money (while making long-term debts) to take subjects not even related to your field, such as Wine Tasting, Wind Sailing, Western Line Dancing, etc., to add to your credits for any degree? Is this supposed to make you more well-rounded, more sophisticated, more mature? The whole system is set up to keep you in school longer so they can make more money. **Schools Are Big Business.**

On top of all this, major universities have a ridiculous amount of unskilled, unlicensed T.A.s (teacher's assistants) to instruct the majority of their students in these useless electives. Many of the T.A.s need not even be college graduates themselves...they could have taken the same course they are now teaching the students only a year or two prior to becoming a T.A.!

All of this has to do with economics. No in-class students, no government funding! The traditional schools get government funding and grants, per student, only if that student is physically there. Therefore, if they told students that they would permit more test challenging (testing what you know about your profession) and that they would permit the use of life experience for legitimate credits (which many schools quietly offer), the average student could then graduate in one-tenth of the time. Most counselors are only aware of the hard way to get a degree, and if they did know an easier way, they wouldn't tell you because they would be putting their own jobs into jeopardy.

For example, an LVN/LPN (licensed vocational nurse/licensed practical nurse) who went to vocational school for eighteen months, with 1/2 of the training done in a hospital, an individual with real, on-the-job experience, with twenty years of hospital and medical experience, earning only $15 to $17 per hour, now has to train newly graduated R.N.s (registered nurses) with less hospital experience than the LVN/LPN. The new R.N. only needs an A.A. Degree and is earning $27 to $30 per hour, with less practicum than the experienced LVN/LPN. Does the working LVN/LPN have the time to sit in a classroom to earn the degree in the traditional fashion? NO! That's not fair!

Think about an engineer who never finished college, but worked for ten to fifteen years at a company. This experienced non-degreed engineer is now helping to train new graduates, who know nothing about the company or its business, and they will shortly be making more money than he does, just because of that mandatory college degree, which is relatively useless against good, on-the-job, life experience in the company. The working engineer does not have the time to sit in a classroom, either, not that they can teach him anything he doesn't already know.

Although you do not need a degree to be good in any profession, unfortunately, it is now mandatory to have a college degree to get the kind of decent job that you want or deserve, as well as to be able to make advancements in your chosen job or career.

Now there is hope. For those of you who are able to afford traditional college and want to enjoy campus life, there are many fine institutions all over the country who will welcome you with open arms. For those of you who feel vocational schools are your best option, there are many schools and financial aid to attend them. Be very careful of fly-by-night schools and schools that cram so much information down you that you just cannot take it all in within the allotted time frame for graduation. Report these schools to the proper authorities so you will not be held liable for a lot of tuition expenses.

Now, for those of you who are on a job or in a career where you have put in some time, and have learned your own and your boss' job (mainly because you are doing a lot of it!), but the lack of a piece of paper (a diploma) is keeping you from advancing, I may be able to direct you to some help. I will direct you to the easiest, the fastest, and the least expensive legal way to get most any degree you wish, except that of being a medical doctor.

There are several non-traditional universities that use your life experiences as the basis for granting credits towards your degree. By not earning your credits in a traditional sit-down school, you can get your degree ten to twelve times faster than in a traditional sit-down school. In the vast majority of industries and occupations, it doesn't matter where you got your legitimate degree. All that matters is that you got it. I hate to burst your bubble, but you can go completely through life without anyone ever asking to see your grade point average!

The following is the U.S. Census Bureau Statistics for 1994 listing the average lifetime earnings based upon a person's educational level:

High School Dropout	$460,000
High School Graduate	756,000
College Dropout	990,000
Bachelor's Degree	1,441,000
Master's Degree	1,989,000
Doctorate Degree	2,460,000

The following are the average costs of traditional sit-down school in order to obtain a degree:

Bachelor's Degree	Average 6 years	$48,000*
Master's Degree	Average 9-1/2 years	72,000*
Doctorate Degree	Average 12 years	96,000*

*plus expenses, not including salaries and years wasted.

You can get a legal, accredited college degree, Bachelor's, Master's, and Doctorate, from many traditional and non-traditional schools through life experience credits and accelerated extension courses. Harvard, Loyola, Pepperdine, and many other colleges have good programs. The programs are based upon awarding credits based upon life experience and test challenging. Their programs allow you to home study. If you have the life experience and can pass the test for your profession, you will earn your degree. It's that simple! The tuitions are low and affordable, and if you cannot pay the whole tuition at once, they offer very good payment plans, so there is no reason why you cannot make plans to earn your degree and advance in your career, or even move to a new career, if you so desire. Take advantage of this opportunity to get ahead, without interrupting your present work schedule.

For the best listings, look on the Internet at www.back2college.com. They have lots of resources available, include listings of schools you can choose from for your degree. Also, there is a book called "College Degrees by Mail and Internet 2000", by John Bear and Mariah Bear. The best accredited undergraduate and graduate schools are listed within this book. You can order this book through any bookstore. Don't forget to go on the Internet and put "college degrees" in the search engine. You'll be surprised at all of the listings you'll pull up!

I am so convinced of the idea of a non-traditional college degree that, if I were a young person thinking about whether or not to go to college, and worrying about the cost, I would decide on the type of business I liked the most, and then I would proceed to get a beginning job with a company in that business. I would study, on my own time, the company and business I was employed in, so that I would know about it inside and out. I would work there approximately 3 to 4 years, advancing if the opportunity presented itself, receiving a salary and the other company benefits which are normally presented to long-term employees, then I would apply to my chosen non-traditional or traditional college. I would present my life experiences and take the test for my profession. Then, I would graduate and receive my college degree. I would use my diploma to make further advancements within my profession possible. If you've already been on a job or in a career for some time, you can definitely get started, **right now**, getting that college degree you deserve. Look into this method, by all means.

Although many lower income students are aware of, and have taken advantage of this avenue, Pell grants and other educational grants are available to assist you in your efforts to attend higher education. The interesting thing about these grants is that they usually **give you more than you actually need** for your school expenses, and are a way for you to obtain an education and **put some extra money into your pocket**, as well. Look into this avenue at your local college or university.

Whichever way you choose to educate yourself, it's very important to realize that education is a lifelong process that doesn't stop at formal schooling. **Never stop learning!**

Notes

Chapter 9

Real Estate on a Budget

*"There is no security on this earth;
there is only opportunity."*
~Douglas MacArthur

At some point, you're going to be interested in possibly owning your own home. If you are able to either increase your income and/or lower your expenses, you also may be able to invest in real estate. You may not believe it is possible, but you can do both on a low income, if you work smarter, not harder.

One way to buy a house on a low income is to buy it directly from the seller, with the seller carrying the mortgage himself. Contrary to popular belief, you don't need a real estate agent to help you buy and sell property. You can learn the ins and outs yourself by reading the excellent real estate investment books available today. Usually, you can buy a very good home in a nice, safe location if you can raise the $2,500 to $5,000 needed for a down payment and costs. Dept. of Housing and Urban Development (HUD) has new low ($500) and no-down programs available for first-time homebuyers in many areas. Call a local Realtor and ask. They will be more than happy to give you all of the information you need on these programs.

You can study the various no-down real estate books available in the libraries and bookstores. They contain various ingenious methods of purchasing property for little or no money down.

In Chapter 12, New Ideas, a new program is mentioned that can help you to buy your own home, as well as investment real estate, for no money down, 100% financing with as low as 3% interest, with up to $5,000,000 available for your real estate needs. No qualifying, no credit needed, no discrimination of any kind. More details on this program are provided in Chapter 12.

You can rent or lease a house with the option to buy. This involves paying the seller an option fee to secure the price and terms of the sale, then paying a bit more on the rent/lease, which is applied towards the down payment. If you do not exercise the option when it expires, you will lose the money you applied towards the down payment and the option fee. If you do exercise the option and buy the house, congratulations! You have just bought a house on the layaway plan! You also got the chance, by living in the home, to make sure that it was worth buying in the first place.

Here's a true winner economically for anyone with the ability to save $300 a month for 36 months (3 years). If you use some of the ideas and resources contained in this book to increase your income and decrease your expenses, you will be able to implement this idea easily.

Suppose you can save $300 per month for 36 months. This will total $10,800, not counting any interest, if you invested the money during this period. Use this money to purchase a 4-unit apartment building in a suburban area with a nice mix of housing available. If you live in one unit of the building, and act as your own resident manager, you can decrease your housing outlay dramatically.

This example assumes that you are comfortable with real estate terms. Ideally, you should study the real estate books available to get comfortable with the figures and terms. **Education, education, education!** This is what this example looks like on paper:

Purchase price on a 4-unit apartment building—$100,000. Down payment 10%—$10,000 (try for a 5% down payment or lower). 3 units x $450 average rent= $1,350/mo. gross income (remember, you will live in one unit rent-free, saving you paying rent somewhere else). $1,350—$660 (mortgage payment on $90,000, financed at 8% interest for 30 years)= $690 left. Property taxes, insurance, and maintenance costs, set aside monthly, should be around 30% (or less) of $1,350, which is $405/mo. $690—$405= $285/mo. net profit. If you close escrow on the building close to the first of the month as possible, preferable from the 1st to the 5th day of the month, you will have the majority of that month's rents, which you could use to help pay for closing costs or miscellaneous costs connect to your purchasing the building. The first payment for the new mortgage isn't due until after one month after closing, and rents are pro-rated, based on the close of escrow. You will also have the tenants' deposits for the apartment building in a savings account, to be transferred to your savings account. The odds are good that your renters will not leave all at one time, so if you have an emergency, the deposits are available to you for a short-term loan. You must pay this back promptly. (Check the local laws regarding your use of renters' deposits.)

If you follow this plan, you now own your first piece of investment property, given yourself an instant increase in income, lowered your expenses (in the form of no rent), and earned valuable tax benefits that will shelter your take-home pay, and give you back that 28% in taxes that the government has been taking from your paycheck.

If you consult your cash flow plan, you are now living rent-free, paying little or no taxes, and bringing in more income, all with one solidly worked plan. This gives you more money to spend, save, and invest, which will greatly reward your thrifty efforts. As an added bonus, you have now locked in your housing costs against the steady bite of inflation, as long as you stay there. (That new program in Chapter 12 is starting to look pretty good!)

You can't afford not to at least give this particular plan a try before knocking it. Many wealthy real estate investors have quietly used this very technique for years to get started on the road to real estate riches!

Notes

Chapter 10

Retirement

*"Goals are as essential to success
as air is to life."*

~David Schwartz

It's never too soon to think about retirement. You may think that age 65 is a long way off into the future, too distant to be concerned about, but actually, the longer you have until retirement, the longer you have to become prepared. The more time it takes until you are age 65, the least amount of money is required to be invested to have a substantial nest egg ready and waiting for you when you get there.

There is no worse fate for a kamikaze pilot than to go through all of the training, then miss the target. That's the fate that will await you if you do not invest for your retirement!

If you are employed at minimum wage for most of your working life, most likely you will not be vested into a pension plan of any kind. Even if you were able to draw upon a pension through your job, who knows if the company, with their pension plan, will still be around by the time of your retirement! Social Security may not be around either by then, and even the government is trying to persuade people to save for retirement on their own. You have to plan as though what you save for yourself is all that you'll have to live on for the rest of your (probably long) life. Don't rely upon anyone else for your well-being! No one is more concerned about you than you. It's time to set goals for your retirement, **right now!**

First off, how much do you think you'll need than? If inflation stays at 4% from now until you retire (highly unlikely), the value of today's $1.00 will likely be equal to $6.00 then. So, if you're living on $1,200 now, $7,200 is what you'll need to equal that standard of living then (we're talking about approximately 30 years from now). Many readers younger than age 35 will watch their $1.00 erode even further. A 20 year-old with 45 years until retirement age may need $29.00 at that time for every $1.00 today. That's scary!

If the value of today's dollar were compared with a 1900 dollar bill, you would find that its value has shrunk by 94%. $1.00 in 1900 value is now worth 6 cents in 1997 value. Whatever you do, you must invest your money to beat inflation rates and taxes!

I believe that the whole economy will also have to rise to the occasion, as it always has in the past, by raising salaries and wages so that the average income keeps up with inflation. But you can't be so certain of our country's ability to keep up with the burden of our national debt load, even with the estimated, inflated budget surpluses. It will likely get harder and harder to make ends meet, especially for a minimum wage earner.

Most likely, people will be working as long as they can before they can retire. The retirement age will probably rise, maybe even to 75 years old. People are living longer. People are already working to make ends meet while they are retired (if they are still healthy enough). What about inflation after retirement? All we can do is the best that we can. It is better to put away as much money for our future benefit as we can and take our chances, than to do nothing and be at the mercy of the government, living in abject poverty.

Most Americans are broke at retirement age. They relied on others for their retirement goals, and never took the time to learn about how to provide a comfortable retirement living for themselves. They just eke by, working full or part-time, collecting what they can from Social Security and a small pension (if they're lucky and have one). They didn't invest in themselves. **You have to invest in yourself in order to do better than this at retirement!**

I may seem to be overly pessimistic at this point, but I've heard too many stories, and life is not usually fair. If something can go wrong, it usually will go wrong. All we can do is face it squarely, and follow our plan to reach our goals. As the saying goes, the best time to plant an oak tree was 20 years ago. The next best time to plant an oak tree is today. Get started planting now!

Here's an amazing observation. If, at age 20, instead of buying an expensive toy or partying like there will be no tomorrow, you invested $13,720, all at one time, and you could get a 10% annual return on your money, allowing it to compound for 45 years, you could take out $8,270 for living expenses every month from age 65 to age 100. If you wanted to be sure that you didn't run out of money if you happened to live longer than 100 years old (there are a lot of folks these days older than 100), just take out $7,970 each month. Remember, inflation will be higher 45 years later, by retirement age. The total principal amount would be $1,000,050, and if this principal is not touched, and continues to compound at 10% annually, that $7,970/mo. would go on forever. Time and compound interest is the key! **Every year that you delay saving makes the goal of a good retirement much, much harder to achieve!**

So now that you know what you are dealing with, you need to look at the best way to accomplish your compounding goal.

There are many ways to invest money for retirement. Pension plans work well for those in secure, stable companies that don't fire people before they are fully vested into their plans. We don't know what Social Security benefits will be available in the future, but it never hurts to find out what you have already accrued during your working years. Contact Social Security at (800) 772-1213 to order Form SSA-7004, Personal Earnings and Benefit Statement (PEBES). When you fill out and return this simple form, you will receive a printout of your Social Security earnings history, with estimates on how much you have paid in Social Security taxes. The printout also shows estimates on the amount of money you would receive if you were to retire today. Social Security has started a new program which mails a copy of your Personal Earnings and Benefit Statement automatically to you every year. Make sure you hold on to this document, and review it for mistakes. Contact Social Security to correct any mistakes. Although you may not have any faith in the system's ability to stay afloat until you retire, it is probably safer to hedge your bets. Even if the requirements to receive monthly Social Security benefits change, there are medical benefits attached that can become important to you if you need medical care after reaching retirement age. My motto is, "Every Little Bit Helps". Work long enough (approximately 10 years) in order to qualify to receive at least the minimum in Social Security benefits in the future. Your well-being during that time may depend on it!

Individual Retirement Accounts (IRAs) are useful as saving tools, and they are tax-deductable. There are many new rules involving IRAs, and new saving products are being introduced. I believe that the best location for your retirement investment funds is into a tax-deferred flexible premium annuity. One benefit is that no taxes are taken out until funds are withdrawn. Annuities are products of life insurance companies which allow you to make monthly or lump-sum investments into an account that will turn around and distribute a set sum of money back to you monthly as a retirement income. In a tax-deferred flexible premium annuity, the minimum contribution to open an account is low (the one I use is only $10), with no limits on the maximum contribution. You can contribute as much as you want, whenever you want. You can withdraw your funds at anytime, but the rules for IRA withdrawals apply here (10% Federal tax penalty if you withdraw any interest or appreciation on the capital before you are 59-1/2 years old, as well as being subject to regular income taxes, at your present tax bracket). You have the ability to invest in several different mutual fund accounts, according to your attitude towards risk. I recommend the American Life Insurance Company of New York, 320 Park Avenue, New York, NY 10022-6839, (800) 872-5963. If you'd like to consider this investment option, give them a call for a prospectus detailing their program.

I have told you everything I presently know about investing for retirement. There are a lot of good books out there that may provide even more insight. Get as much information as you can, then get started. **Don't wait any longer!**

To reiterate the rules for investing, these are the most important:

*Be absolutely convinced of the need to save on a regular basis.

*Begin investing as soon as possible!

*Start investing with the largest amount of money you can.

*Look for the highest rate of return you feel you can safely achieve on your money over time.

My hope is that you will have great success in the growth of your retirement nest egg!

Notes

Chapter 11

Health

*"No man is free who is
not master of himself."*

~Epictetus

Most people would think that "Health" would be a strange topic in a
financial book, but our health definitely affects our pocketbook in a big
way. Smoking, immoderate alcohol use, and drug use are expensive
vices, and should not be a part of your cash flow plan, especially if children are a part of your household. I realize that you are an adult, and you
have every right to indulge in whatever you feel like doing to yourself,

but there are reasons why it is not always good to do whatever you want to do. The money you spend today on expensive vices cripples your saving and earning power, just as if you were paying more in taxes. Life insurance will be hard to obtain and more expensive. You may get sick more often, and carry the illness longer. Your children may become ill from second-hand smoke or be born with health problems, and need more medical care than normal, which is very expensive. Years of physical abuse of your body will take its toll one day, when you can least afford to handle it. It's just not worth the headaches and expenses. There are many programs available to help you to quit bad health habits. Use them to your benefit! Don't ignore your health! It's more valuable than any monetary wealth you may gather. **Your health is the most valuable asset you already possess!**

Here are some suggestions on how to ease the stress of daily living, and ways to give your body and mind a boost:

*Take a good multi-vitamin supplement. Most of us don't eat right.

*Start a program of moderate exercise. One of the best exercises is walking.

*Make an effort to eat properly. We need good fuel, just like our cars.

*Listen to calming relaxation tapes.

*Take an hour for yourself every day.

*Get a physical exam once a year. If you don't have medical insurance, go to a low-cost medical clinic.

*Buy yourself flowers. Don't wait for someone else to do it for you.

*Take 5 minutes to relax your back, neck, and facial muscles. Focus on each area one at a time. Exhale, and try to consciously relax that part of your body.

*Give yourself a massage with a good, thick, fragrant lotion after a long, hot soak in the tub. It's a good stress reliever.

*Learn to meditate. There are good books in the library on the subject.

*Find a moment every day to think about what you have to be grateful for.

Notes

Chapter 12

New Ideas

*"Don't compete. Create. Find out
what everyone else is doing and
then, don't do it."*

~Joel Weldon

There is always room for brainstorming for the future millionaire on a mission. When you have less money to work with, you have to become more creative about how you get it, and about how you use it. The ideas I came up with are not new in themselves, but they are not being used to their fullest extent. If they were, I believe that there would be more financially-secure people in our society.

*New Idea Number One: I've mentioned this program earlier in this book, and now I will give you a little more detail about it. The program is called "The 12 Month Advantage Plan". This Plan will provide you with an unsecured, no-qualifying loan of either $10,000 or $20,000 (depending on the membership you choose), at 6% interest, amortized for 15 years, no credit necessary. Under the Basic Membership, you would receive a loan of $10,000, and you would be provided with a one-year's paid membership into Home Equity Associates, an Australian non-profit cooperative organization that can help you to live your dream of financial security through their real estate financing projects. Under the Premiere Membership, you would receive a loan of $20,000, and you would be provided with a one-year's paid membership into Home Equity Associates, as well. You may use your Home Equity Associates membership to buy your own home, and to invest in residential rental property, with 100% financing, for as low as 3% interest. You will be eligible to borrow up to $5,000,000. Just think of the possibilities! For more information on "The 12 Month Advantage Plan", contact Holosa Co. at (877) 477-3246, or on the Internet at www.holosa.com.

*New Idea Number Two: Cooperative Living. Get together with a few families who share your attitudes and compatibilities. Elect a financial decision group to organize and coordinate the financial endeavors you plan to share. You can either pool together and buy an apartment building for all of the families to live in, or you can continue to live apart, but the actual aim of a cooperative living situation is to pool together resources for the betterment of all involved. As it is said, two heads are better than one, and, in some cases, more heads may even be better. The group would decide upon what the goals of this arrangement would be (i.e. cheaper rates on bulk buying, cheaper housing costs, investing for retirement as a group, the elimination of debt for all members, etc.). In short, your goals can be anything you can think of that might benefit from group participation. It is a known fact that it is less expensive to live comfortably if there are several cash flows to pull from.

Cooperative living should only be attempted by like-minded, mature, dedicated people who are creative and greatly enjoy each other's company. Therefore, cooperative living is not recommended for people of the same family, unless your family enjoys a closer relationship with each other than the majority of families today. This idea is not for everyone, so be honest with yourselves about whether your personalities can handle this type of arrangement.

*New Idea Number Three: Family Savings. This concept is hardly ever used, but it can really defuse family tensions about money-lending when one or more members are in need. First, get together for a family discussion. Every member of the family has different financial needs at different times. The usual method followed by most families is for everyone to run to Mom, Dad, Grandma, Grandpa, Aunt, Uncle, etc., looking for a quick loan. There are many reasons to need quick cash that you can pay back, but, sometimes, there is no one available who can help you that quick. All of the family members involved should agree to fund a bank savings account with a small amount of money every month, let's say $25 each. This monthly $25 should be treated by everyone as a regular bill, money spent from their budget. Mom and Dad should definitely contribute to the family savings, for their own piece of mind.

If a family of four contributes $25 each per month, the savings account (kept by a responsible person, such as Mom or Dad) would gain $100 per month. There will be normal periods when there will not be any crises that will need cash to solve, but there will always come a time when someone will have a cash emergency. A quick family discussion, either in person or over the phone, should decide whether the situation merits taking money out of the family savings to help the needy family member. Of course, if someone messes up unnecessarily, there should be some discussion about responsibility and taking care of business correctly. But the fact that the needy family member **has** been contributing to the family savings means that they are entitled to some help, which is the main reason why they have been contributing monthly, in the first place.

If the family savings grows regularly, and any borrowed money is paid back, there will always be enough available to help any contributing family member in need. If the fund grows to over $1,000, invest the continuing contributions into a mutual fund. I'm sure that your family will appreciate the ease in which they can ask for money, without the usual tension, guilt, and arguments (I hope!).

*New Idea Number Four: Opportunity Grants. Get together 5 individuals and/or families. Five is the important number, no more, no less. The object is to provide each of the five partners with a $5,000 opportunity grant, which they can do whatever they want with. The money can be used for investments, savings, travel, as a down payment for a home or real estate purchase, a car, etc. To implement this plan, a contribution of $200 per month must be made by each of the 5 partners for renewable periods of 25 months each. Draw up a contract to emphasize and legalize the commitment. For the first 5 months, $200 from each partner will accrue, adding up to $1,000 each month, for a total of $5,000 in those 5 months. Draw straws, cast lots, roll dice, etc., in order to determine the granting order (i.e. who gets the grant first, second, third, fourth, and fifth). On the fifth month, give the first $5,000 grant to the first grantee. Then, continue the next month with the usual $200 contributions, including the receiver of the first grant. Follow the same procedure, distributing $5,000 every 5th month, down to the fifth grantee. Give them their $5,000 grant and stop. This is the end of the 25-month period. Decide if you want to continue with the program again. If you do, make a new granting order, preferably reverse order, allowing the fifth grantee to become the first, etc. (that's only fair) to change the positions of the partners, and form a new contract for the new commitment.

The beauty of this program is its simplicity. The first grantee will have paid their $5,000 by the time of the fifth grant. The fifth grantee has paid in advance for their $5,000 grant. The grants in-between are paid for before and after they are received by the grantees. The whole process is actually a forced savings program. If $200/mo. is too much, try $100, which will make a $2,500 grant. If a partner has trouble participating in the middle of the program, they can either borrow the money to keep up their commitment from someone else until they can get over their rough patch, or they can let someone else buy them out (i.e. pay the leaving partner the amount they have put in already, then take their place). Honesty is the main point of this plan.

For this program to be effective, every partner must treat this obligation seriously. Don't participate in the program if you are in the slightest way doubtful that you can keep this obligation up! It is not fair to the other partners if one messes up the program unnecessarily.

These ideas are only the beginning of what can be done, if you use creativity to achieve your goals. Use your imagination, and think of new possibilities!

Afterword

I would like to share my little fantasy with you. I hope that this book can affect enough people so that there will be a financial revolution that changes the financial course of our nation. (This is a LITTLE fantasy?!) If everyone could get a copy of this book, and decide to implement the simple steps to financial independence described within these pages, there wouldn't be a need for a Social Security program; everyone would live comfortably, and everyone would have an enjoyable retirement, something they could look forward to, doing exactly what they wanted to do, 365 days a year; and, when people passed away, they would leave a great monetary and fiscal inheritance to their children, and their children's children. There would be no more poverty, and happy, satisfied people would make a happier, more satisfied world, which would create a better place for all of us to live in.

This is my fantasy, and, by writing this book, I am trying to do my little part to make my fantasy come true!

Conclusions

I hope that you were able to obtain some needed nuggets of financial wisdom from these pages. I have tried to condense into this book volumes and volumes of financial information into a concise, easy-to-read format for those of you who are not very familiar with financial terms and concepts. I hope that I succeeded with this task, and didn't confuse you further. If you need more information about finances, or you just want to do more research on the subject, there is a list of books in the "References" section of this book that I suggest you read to further your education in finance and the use of money.

I believe that I stayed within my basic premise, which was to show you how to become financially healthy, wealthy, and wise on a minimum wage income. My examples were based upon the $5.15/hr. minimum wage, even allowing for taxes. Any examples given using amounts over minimum wage can be accounted for by the assumption that the investor is earning more money through a part-time income, over and above their normal wages, in order to supplement their wages for their investment project goals.

Let's look at a brief overview of what I am trying to help you to accomplish with each chapter:

*In Chapter One, Real Life Cash Flow, you need to get serious about your financial status. Make a cash flow plan. Look at your income and expenses, and get rid of any expenses that are unnecessary and unproductive. If you have a family, protect your family with Term life insurance. Include saving and investing for the future in your cash flow plan.

*In Chapter Two, Investing on a Budget, the nuts and bolts of investing are described. You can see for yourself how you can make the money that you have worked so hard for, now work for you, through time and compound interest.

*In Chapter Three, Credit, if credit debt is stopping you from saving and investing, get rid of it! It's no longer a status symbol to have a ton of credit cards and a load of debt. Secured credit cards can build a good credit record, since a good credit record can be an advantage in this society.

*In Chapter Four, Bankruptcy, there is an explanation of bankruptcy and how to obtain it, if your credit situation is out of control. Bankruptcy is perfectly legal, and it is the best way you can make a fresh start, if you are having serious credit problems.

*In Chapter Five, Value Hints, there are suggestions that should help you to become more thrifty, and can show you how to make the most out of each dollar.

*In Chapter Six, Money Smarts, you can use these suggestions to maximize your cash flow by increasing your income, and/or decreasing your expenses.

*In Chapter Seven, Entertainment on a Budget, there are various low-cost activities that you can use to have fun, especially on a tight budget. Always take the time to have fun!

*In Chapter Eight, Schooling and Careers, our present educational system is exposed for what it is and what it isn't, and options to this system are presented that may help you to get ahead in your education and career.

*In Chapter Nine, Real Estate, various ways to own a home and residential income property are presented.

*In Chapter Ten, Retirement, there is an explanation of retirement options, estimates on inflation for the future, and how it can affect your retirement, and ways to invest for your retirement nest egg.

*In Chapter Eleven, Health, there are suggestions on how you can ease the stress of daily living, and the advice given to make you think about making the effort to gain control over any bad habits, which can cost you plenty, both physically and financially over time.

*In Chapter Twelve, New Ideas, there are four interesting economic concepts that may help you to gain greater prosperity and more control over your finances.

Finally, only you know what you really want out of life. Only you can ultimately decide to take control of your life, from others, and learn how to steer your ship, by yourself. All it takes is a little determination, a little persistence, and a little know-how, and you can be on your way to becoming financially healthy, wealthy, and wise!

Since you now have the answers to your financial questions in your hands, **why don't you get started on the road to your success, TODAY?**

Lorianne Holt
September 16, 2000

References

Allen, Robert G.—Creating Wealth; Simon and Schuster

Allen, Robert G.—Nothing Down for the '90s: How to Buy Real Estate with Little or No Money Down; Simon and Schuster

Bottom Line Yearbook 1996; Boardroom Classics

Levine, Karen—Keeping Life Simple; Storey Communications, Inc.

Long, Charles—How to Survive Without a Salary; Warwick Publishing

McAleese, Tama—Get Rich Slow; Career Press

Porter, Sylvia—Sylvia Porter's Your Finances in The 1990s; Simon and Schuster

Stowers, James E.—Yes You Can...Achieve Financial Independence; Deer Publishing

About the Author

Lorianne Holt is a financial advisor who has compiled most of the information found in this book from her own life experiences and research.

Ms. Holt is an avid reader (especially of financial books), and has always wanted to write a book to help others, so this book was created to share her financial wisdom with others. Some of the knowledge Ms. Holt has acquired for this book was gathered during her past experiences of trying to raise a young family of six children, as a single parent struggling to make ends meet, and while surviving on welfare for a time.

Ms. Holt brings a matter-of-fact viewpoint to this book, based upon her belief that anyone with the right determination and drive can succeed in this world, and get what they want out of this life, especially in the United States.

Ms. Holt lives with her partner, Ruth Sanchez, and with their six children: Angalina, Stephany, Bryan, Anthony, Jenefer, and Matthew. Their seventh child, Kimberli, lives nearby. The whole family lives in beautiful Southern California.